Forest Fire!

Dennis Fertig

Jody Lyle

Won

Victor

Beth

Rigby®

A Harcourt Achieve Imprint

www.Rigby.com
1-800-531-5015

What do you think
a forest fire looks like?

We know that forest
fires are bad for people,
plants, and animals.

Forest fires change
the earth.

They destroy trees
and animals' homes.

They put campers,
hikers, and
firefighters in danger.

You might also be surprised to know that there are good forest fires!

Won, Victor, and Beth are asking Jody Lyle, a **park ranger**, to tell them about forest fires.

Won: *Ranger Lyle, what causes forest fires?*

Ranger Lyle: A fire must have **fuel**, air, and heat to burn.
Trees, bushes, and grasses are fuel in a forest.

Trees and air are always in forests, but heat comes from **nature** or people.

5

Victor: *How does nature start fires?*

Ranger Lyle: Heat from **lightning** starts fires by making trees, bushes, or grasses burn.

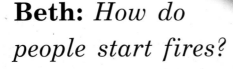

 **Beth:** *How do people start fires?*

 Ranger Lyle: When people are careless with matches or campfires, a fire can start.
A power tool or an electric wire can also start a fire.

Some people set fires on purpose.

Beth: *Why do people set forest fires on purpose?*

 Ranger Lyle: Sometimes people set fires for bad reasons. Park rangers also start fires for good reasons.

 Victor: *Why do park rangers set forest fires?*

 Ranger Lyle: Sometimes they set forest fires that are good. They burn the dead wood in the forest and make openings where new trees can grow.

9

Won: *How do firefighters put out forest fires?*

Ranger Lyle: Firefighters drop something that looks like red water from an airplane to stop fires.

This makes trees and bushes harder to burn.

Ranger Lyle: Firefighters also take away the fire's fuel by making a **fireline**.

A fireline looks like a wide dirt road.

Beth: *How do firefighters make a fireline?*

Ranger Lyle: They cut trees and take away the dead wood, bushes, and grasses.

Smoke jumpers are firefighters who jump from airplanes into the forest to make firelines.

Victor: *How can people help park rangers and firefighters?*

Ranger Lyle: Scientists help park rangers and firefighters. They use computers to see where lightning strikes and where fires may start.

Other people can help by being careful with matches and campfires. We can all take care of our parks and forests.

Won, Victor, and Beth: Thanks, Ranger Lyle!

Glossary

firefighters people who put out fires

fireline a wide piece of land around a forest fire that firefighters clear of trees, brush, and dead wood

fuel something like trees or bushes that can burn when air and heat are added

lightning a flash of electricity in the air

park ranger a person who works to protect a park or a forest

scientists people who know science and study it